Legends of the Bible: The Life and Legacy of the Prophet Jeremiah

By Charles River Editors

Michelangelo's painting of Jeremiah on the Sistine Chapel

About Charles River Editors

Charles River Editors was founded by Harvard and MIT alumni to provide superior editing and original writing services, with the expertise to create digital content for publishers across a vast range of subject matter. In addition to providing original digital content for third party publishers, Charles River Editors republishes civilization's greatest literary works, bringing them to a new generation via ebooks.

Introduction

Rembrandt's painting of Jeremiah after the fall of Jerusalem (1630)

Jeremiah

"And when your people say, 'Why has the Lord our God done all these things to us?' you shall say to them, 'As you have forsaken me and served foreign gods in your land, so you shall serve foreigners in a land that is not yours.'" – Jeremiah 5:19

A lot of ink has been spilled covering the lives of history's most influential figures, but how much of the forest is lost for the trees? In Charles River Editors" Legends of the Bible series, readers can get caught up to speed on the lives of the Bible's most important men and women in the time it takes to finish a commute, while learning interesting facts long forgotten or never known.

The belief in prophets is as old as religion itself, and the tradition of prophets is especially prevalent in Judaism and Christianity, with prophets like Isaiah and Jeremiah being among the most famous historical figures in the Bible. In addition to interpreting and sharing the word of God with the people, ancient prophets also served a variety of different roles in the Bible. God had prophets like Jeremiah perform symbolic acts that foretold future events, particularly hardships that the Israelites suffered at the hands of the Babylonians and Egyptians. The abilities of the prophets to predict future events have become the primary ways in which contemporary society remembers them, which has ensured that the term prophet (which meant spokesman in Hebrew) is now part of the lexicon and means something far different than the ancient definitions.

The prophet Jeremiah was born into a time of great political and religious turmoil for Judah. Longstanding institutions were being overturned left and right, and leaders scrambled for power amidst the ensuing chaos. In the century before Jeremiah was born, Assyria was the prominent political power that dominated Judean life and politics. Judah was fortunate enough not to suffer the fate of their northern neighbor Israel, which was overthrown and resettled by Sargon II in 720 B.C., but the angst that the Judeans felt living under the thumb of the Assyrians comes through clearly in the oracles of 8th century Judean prophets like Micah, Amos and Isaiah of Jerusalem.

Around the time Jeremiah was born (627 B.C.), an Assyrian official in Babylon, Nabopolassar, led the Babylonians in a revolt against their Assyrian oppressors and succeeded in reclaiming Babylon for the Babylonians. This successful act of rebellion against Assyria created shockwaves of aspirations that reverberated throughout all of the Assyrian vassal states, including Judah. The events around Jeremiah ensured that he would undergo some of the Bible's most famous trials and tribulations and also rub shoulders with some of the most famous figures of the ancient world, including the Babylonian king Nebuchadnezzar II. Not surprisingly, he has been credited as the author of a few books in the Bible.

Legends of the Bible: The Life and Legacy of the Prophet Jeremiah discusses the life, history, stories, and Scripture passages about the famous prophet, examining the Bible and historical record to piece together an understanding of his life. Along with pictures and a bibliography, you will learn about the prophet Jeremiah like you never have before, in no time at all.

Chapter 1: Background to Jeremiah's Life

Jeremiah's life was dominated by the geopolitical situation in Mesopotamia, but political life was not the only area of life where major disruptions were taking place. In the decades before Jeremiah's birth, Manasseh ruled Judah as the longest ruling king in its history, and one of the ways that Manasseh procured such a lengthy reign was by completely acquiescing to the demands of the Assyrians. One aspect of this stance entailed incorporating the worship of the Assyrian religious pantheon into Judean cultic life, including worship of the Assyrians' chief deity Aššur, the goddess Ištar, and multiple astral deities.

There were two major religious schools of thought in Judah at this time. The syncretistic Yahwists, who believed that it was perfectly acceptable to worship other deities alongside YHWH, supported Manasseh. The strict Yahwists, who believed that worshippers of YHWH could worship no other gods besides YHWH, had supported Hezekiah, Manasseh's father. With that said, it's important to remember that there were not yet any groups espousing the idea that YHWH was the only deity that existed. The existence of other gods during the 8th and 7th centuries in Judah was a given. It was only with the preaching of Isaiah of Babylon (also known as Second Isaiah or Deutero-Isaiah) in the 6th century that this new monotheistic perspective would come into play.

Hezekiah, Manasseh, and Amon

The strict Yahwists despised Manasseh, but his royal entourage was so infused with Assyrian administrators that no opportunity would be afforded the strict Yahwists to depose him. These strict Yahwists simply bided their time until Amon, Manasseh's son, finally succeeded him to the throne. Sensing their opportunity, the strict Yahwists infiltrated Amon's royal court, and only two years after his coronation they orchestrated a coup and had Amon assassinated (2 Kgs. 21:23). Calling themselves "the people of the land" this group of strict Yahwists then turned on their patsies in the royal court, executing them for their treachery and thereby conveniently eliminating any evidence of the conspiracy and the involvement of "the people of the land" (2 Kgs. 21:24). Positioning themselves as the restorers of justice, "the people of the land" then installed the eight-year old Josiah as king, while they acted as his "advisors" on matters of state.

However, as Josiah grew older, he was no longer as pliable as he was in the early years of his reign. Although they had trained him as a strict Yahwist, "the people of the land" wanted more control than they already had. They decided the best course of action was to create a forgery. They had already created a document (Deut. 12-26) that they had used as the program for the reforms they had carried out during the reign of Hezekiah, but they realized that simply presenting this program to Josiah as the basis for what they had carried out with Hezekiah would hold very little sway with Josiah. They needed to infuse it with more authority.

The solution was to embed the prior program that had not mentioned Moses at all within a series of farewell speeches delivered by Moses prior to entering the land (Deut. 4:44-11:32; 28:1-35, 38-68). These speeches would take the form of an Assyrian vassal treaty. Having raised Josiah and acted as his trusted advisors for so many years, they knew that psychologically this combination would have the greatest impact on Josiah. In their education of Josiah, they had ensured that he had the utmost respect for Moses, the founding figure of Yahwistic religion. As an Assyrian vassal himself, Josiah had read multiple vassal treaties in his last 15 years or so as king. The antiquity of Moses, combined with the authority of the vassal treaty format, would be too great for Josiah to ignore.

"The people of the land," called "Deuteronomists" by scholars precisely because of this document, set about creating this elaborate forgery. They gathered ancient-looking parchment and practiced writing in an archaic-looking script. They then carefully drafted the scroll, and in 622 B.C., they hid it in the temple of YHWH. One day, one of the temple servants was cleaning up and noticed an old dust covered scroll that he had never noticed before. He opened it, read several lines, and became excited. He brought it to the high priest, Hilkiah, who studied the script and the parchment and determined it was authentic. When Shaphan, the secretary of the king, came to Hilkiah for the purposes of financial accounting, Hilkiah mentioned to Shaphan that he had found "the book of the Law" in the temple and gave Shaphan the opportunity to read it himself (2 Kgs. 22:3-8). When Shaphan returned to the palace from his financial accounting trip, he carried the "ancient" scroll with him and read it aloud to Josiah, in addition to passing on what he had learned about its provenance from the high priest, Hilkiah.

The ruse worked like a charm, and Josiah immediately accepted the document as authoritative, implementing its stipulations wherever he could. Jeremiah would have been around 5 years old when the scroll was found and the reform movement began.

Chapter 2: The Sources for Jeremiah's Life

Icon of the Prophet Jeremiah

In the case of Jeremiah, the book that bears his name in the Hebrew Bible is the primary source for information on the prophet's life. There are a few other minor sources, but these are certainly peripheral.

The book of Jeremiah falls second in the "Prophets" section of the Hebrew Bible, which is ordered by book length according to chapter number. Thus, for example, Isaiah has 66 chapters compared with Jeremiah's 52 chapters. The Talmud preserves an older order (before chapter divisions) that places Jeremiah first, and Jeremiah runs ten pages longer than Isaiah in the Hebrew Bible (in the *Biblia Hebraica Stuttgartensia*). This makes Jeremiah the most prolific of the Hebrew prophets, even more so since only the first third of the book of Isaiah comes from Isaiah of Jerusalem.

Unlike the book of Isaiah, the book of Jeremiah is not limited to prophetic oracles and speeches attributed to the prophet. The contents of the book of Jeremiah can be roughly divided into three categories: 1) short first person poetic sayings attributed to the prophet (most of chs. 1-25; possibly 46-51); 2) third person reports about Jeremiah or his message (19:1-20:6; 26-29; 37-44); and 3) long first person prose speeches provided with third person headings (1:4-10; 11; 18; 21; 25; 32; 34; 35). This last category is interspersed at various thematic section breaks in the text, and the vocabulary differs from that of the first two categories.

It is often difficult for modern readers to read the prophetic books with any type of clarity or coherence. Readers can become lost moving from one oracle to the next, and one gets the sense that there is not even a train of thought to be followed. In fact, this haphazard impression of the Hebrew prophetic books appears more clearly with Jeremiah than with any other prophetic book. However, most scholars agree that the book of Jeremiah is not a single book or scroll but rather a collection of different books or scrolls centered around the prophet Jeremiah. The first discernible book within these books consists of chapters 1-20. A nice inclusio "coming forth from the womb" ties these chapters together appearing at the beginning (1:5) and at the end (20:18) of this original scroll.

The ancient editors themselves disagreed over how the book of Jeremiah should be organized. Most English translations follow the Hebrew ordering with chapter divisions and versification. The Septuagint, a 2nd or 3rd century Greek translation of the Hebrew text, has a completely different order for the text, shown in the chart below. Not only does the Greek text appear in a significantly different order, but the Greek text is also shorter, nearly 1/8th shorter than the Hebrew text. As early as the 4th century, the Christian theologian Jerome accused the Septuagint translators of shortening and abbreviating the original Hebrew text (*Prologue to Jeremiah*, Pl. 24, col. 679). On the other hand, in the 19th and early 20th centuries, some scholars began to suggest that perhaps the Greek Septuagint represented an earlier Hebrew original, and that the traditional Masoretic Hebrew text contained additions and changes in its order.

It was not until the discovery of the Dead Sea Scrolls in the 1940's that the arguments of these scholars were given real teeth. Among the biblical texts found among the Dead Sea Scrolls were six scrolls of the book of Jeremiah. Two of these manuscripts aligned closely with the longer Masoretic text (4QJer[a] dated to circa 200 B.C. and 4QJer[c] dated to circa 25 B.C.), but two others (4QJer[b] and 4QJer[d], which both dated to circa 150 B.C.) were much more in line with the Septuagint translation. This discovery pretty well shut the lid on the traditional view of the two different versions first espoused by Jerome.

Bartolomeo Cavarozzi's painting of Jerome being visited by angels.

One very interesting suggestion that breathes a good deal of life into this otherwise dry problem completely sidesteps the question of which version was original and which was the later redaction. A standard practice with ancient texts was the addition of the colophon, which was something like the signature of the scribe who edited or wrote a particular text. Scholar Jack R. Lundbom has pointed out that the shorter Old Greek version (a precursor to the Septuagint) ends with Jeremiah addressing his scribe Baruch ben Neriah (ch. 45 in English versions, which appears in 51:31-35 in the Septuagint). He argues that this ending acts as an ancient colophon. From this he further extrapolates that Baruch compiled this shorter edition in Egypt, where he was taken captive with Jeremiah (Jer. 43:5-7). In Baruch's edition, the oracles against foreign nations appear immediately after 25:13a in no discernible order, the king of Babylon was never named, Jeremiah and Hananiah are simply named without an accompanying title, and the prophetic oracles rarely begin with "thus says YHWH".

The longer Masoretic text, on the other hand, concludes with Jeremiah addressing Baruch's brother, Seraiah ben Neraiah (51:59-64). Lundbom argues that Seraiah compiled this edition in Babylon, where he was taken captive. Seraiah chose to place the oracles against foreign nations at the end of the collection and arranged them in geographical order from west to east ending with Babylon, he called the king of Babylon by name (Nebuchadnezzar), he included the title "prophet" with every mention of Jeremiah and Hananiah, and he introduced many of Jeremiah's oracles with the phrase "thus says YHWH". It would have been possible for any editor in

Babylon to make these changes, but the compelling factor behind this theory is that there are many substantive differences that could not have been made by just any editor in Babylon. Seraiah added an entire oracle (33:14-26) that was not present in Baruch's edition. He also provided accurate patronymics for the prophets Ahab and Zedekiah (29:21) that would not have been readily available to any Babylonian editor.

One of the most interesting features of Seraiah's Babylonian edition is the use of ciphers to refer to Babylonia and the Chaldeans. Presumably, whereas Baruch could write oracles of judgment unabashedly about Babylonia and the Chaldeans while in Egypt, such a practice would not be smart for one in Babylon. Because of this concern, Seraiah disguised Jeremiah's original prophecies with an atbash cipher. This term consists of the first letter of the alphabet (*aleph*), followed by the last letter of the alphabet (*taw*), and then the second letter of the alphabet (*beth*) followed by the second to last letter of the alphabet (*shin*). In other words, the scribe writes the alphabet in one column alongside the inverted alphabet in the other column. The letters in the first column are then substituted for the letters in the second column. In English, this would mean "z" would stand for the letter "a" and "y" would stand for the letter "b", etc.

Several other books have been inappropriately attributed to Jeremiah. In the Talmud, the rabbis took note of the duplication of the narrative report that appears at the end of Kings (2 Kgs. 25) and at the end of Jeremiah (ch. 52). The conclusion they drew from this was that Jeremiah was the author of both the book of Kings and the book of Jeremiah. While most modern scholars would not entertain this thought, Mark Leuchter has argued that Jeremiah was himself trained as a Deuteronomistic scribe.

The book most universally attributed to Jeremiah, aside from the book of Jeremiah, is the book of Lamentations. The superscription to the book of Lamentations contained in the Septuagint reads as follows: "And it came to pass, after Israel had been carried away captive, and Jerusalem had become desolate, that Jeremiah sat weeping, and lamented with this lamentation over Jerusalem, saying…" The Talmud, the Aramaic Targum of Jonathan, Origen, and Jerome all attributed Lamentations to Jeremiah. The Septuagint also connects this book with Jeremiah in the canonical order that it assigns to the books: Jeremiah, Baruch, Lamentations, the Epistle of Jeremiah. In the Hebrew Bible, Jeremiah was ordered with the Latter Prophets, whereas Lamentations was included with the Writings. The source of the tradition contained in the Septuagint superscription is likely the statement in Chronicles, "Jeremiah also uttered a lament for Josiah, and all the singing men and singing women have spoken of Josiah in their laments to this day. They made these a custom in Israel; they are recorded in the Laments." (2 Chr. 35:25, NRSV). Jeremiah has largely been remembered as the "weeping prophet" due to Lamentations.

Modern scholars have been fairly adamant that the book of Lamentations should be considered an anonymous collection of poems in the Hebrew Bible and not attributed to Jeremiah, but unlike many parallel cases, the negative evidence on this score is slim indeed. Linguistic studies comparing the grammar and vocabulary of the two books have proved inconclusive, and the Hebrew is typical of the early 6th century, when Jeremiah was writing. One example of the floundering nature of the evidence in this regard comes from the late Delbert Hillers. Hillers was the W. W. Spence Professor of Semitic Languages at Johns Hopkins University until he retired in 1994, and he published extensively on both the Hebrew Prophets and the book of Lamentations until he died in 1999. If there was any scholar with the requisite background to bring the most persuasive arguments against the authorship of Lamentations by Jeremiah, it would be Hillers. His three main points of contention are: the reference to aid from Egypt (Lam 4:17); the reference to YHWH forbidding nations to enter the Jerusalem sanctuary (Lam. 1:10 vs. Jer. 7:14); and the reference to prophets receiving no vision from YHWH (Lam. 2:9).

Hillers' first point would be quite compelling, given Jeremiah's pro-Babylonian stance noted throughout this text, but when one actually reads Lamentations 4:17, there is no reference to Egypt specifically at all: "Our eyes failed, ever watching vainly for help; we were watching eagerly for a nation that could not save." The lament expresses a corporate hope that some other nation would come to their aid (and under Josiah, Judah was certainly looking to Egypt), but this does not seem to run counter to Jeremiah's message. Even if Egypt is the intended reference here, Egypt is not portrayed in a positive light, and it would not seem to be much of a stretch to think that Jeremiah could identify with the hopes of his contemporaries in a "we" statement even if he himself had not entertained the same hope.

Hiller's second point, regarding a prohibition against foreign nations entering the sanctuary, is an integral part of Deuteronomic law upon which Jeremiah was dependent. The text to which Hillers refers (Lam 1:10) contains references not only the "sanctuary," but also the "congregation/assembly." In Deuteronomy 23:3, part of the text with which Jeremiah was intimately familiar, there is a law preventing the "Ammonite and Moabite" from entering the "assembly" of the Lord, where the same vocabulary is used in both cases. This is exactly the type of intertextual commentary with Deuteronomy that Jeremiah uses throughout his text. Just because Jeremiah prophesied that YHWH would punish Judah by defiling the temple does not mean that Jeremiah would not have maintained that there was a law prohibiting foreigners from the "assembly of YHWH." It actually assumes the fact.

Hillers' third and final point is that it makes no sense to him that Jeremiah would say, "Her prophets find no vision from YHWH" (Lam. 2:9, NRSV) since this would imply that his own visions are not from YHWH. But Jeremiah makes this same accusation to his contemporaries on numerous occasions. "On that day, says YHWH, courage shall fail the king and the officials; the priests shall be appalled and the prophets astounded" (Jer. 4:9, NRSV). "The prophets are nothing but wind, for the word is not in them" (Jer. 5:13, NRSV). In this way Jeremiah frequently criticized the "prophets" with this term, even though he clearly excluded himself. There is no reason to think that the passage in Lamentations would need to be read any differently.

These points are meant in no way to take away from Hillers' scholarship but rather to highlight just how tenuous the evidence against Jeremiah's authorship of Lamentations truly is. For modern scholars, judging later attributions of authorship as secondary and incorrect is so commonplace that it almost becomes the default position. While the points made against Hiller are not an argument that Lamentations is authentic material from Jeremiah, they point out that in this case, it's just as difficult to prove Lamentations was not written by Jeremiah.

This is not the case with the other "additions to Jeremiah" that are clearly later in origin. The book of Baruch contains an interesting variant tradition discussed in the chapter about Jeremiah's Fate. The Epistle/Letter of Jeremiah is a separate book from Baruch in the Septuagint, with Lamentations separating the two. In Jerome's Vulgate (Latin translation), however, the Epistle of Jeremiah becomes chapter 6 of Baruch. Despite its misleading title, the book is neither a letter nor written by the prophet Jeremiah. The tradition that Jeremiah had composed a letter and sent it to Babylon is found in Jeremiah 29, and it is this tradition upon which the superscription to the Epistle of Jeremiah depends. This superscription is the only part of the work that would suggest it is a letter. Otherwise, it is just a long satire against idols and idolatry originally written in Hebrew.

Unlike some of the other apocryphal texts, where Hebrew copies were found either among the Nag Hammadi corpus or the Dead Sea Scrolls, the Epistle of Jeremiah is only extant in Greek. One small, badly damaged papyrus (pap7QEpJer gr) among the Dead Sea Scrolls has been identified as belonging to the Epistle of Jeremiah (v. 44), but it is in Greek. The only way scholars can be sure that the text was originally written in Hebrew is that the author was clearly dependent on the precursor to the Masoretic Hebrew version of Jeremiah, rather than the precursor to the Greek Septuagint version.

Finally, in terms of sources, additional mention should be made of the Syriac Apocalypse of Baruch (also known as 2 Baruch) and the Greek Apocalypse of Baruch (3 Baruch). These works are far removed both in time and in thought and content from the prophet Jeremiah and are thus of less concern.

Chapter 3: Jeremiah's Family

In the days of King David, there were two priests, Abiathar and Zadok, who figure prominently in the stories concerning David. But after David died, Solomon banished Abiathar to Anathoth for conspiring with Adonijah to usurp the throne from Solomon (1 Kgs. 2:26). The general scholarly consensus is that Jeremiah was a descendent of Abiathar who grew up as a priest in Anathoth (Jer. 1:1). This means that Jeremiah grew up in a priestly family not connected with the temple.

There are two important repercussions based on Jeremiah's lack of connection to the temple. The first relates to an exaggerated importance placed on non-temple related cultic activities, like the singing of psalms. Coupled with this perspective is a second, bound up in the first, that these latter activities are more important than the performance of temple rituals, like sacrifices. It is for this reason that Jeremiah can say:

> "Of what use to me is frankincense that comes from Sheba,
>> or sweet cane from a distant land?
> Your burnt offerings are not acceptable,
>> nor are your sacrifices pleasing to me." (Jer. 6:20, NRSV)

Later in his career, however, the people of Anathoth turned on the prophet Jeremiah, which is why some scholars believe that the material in 12:1-6 actually chronologically precedes that in 11:18-23:

> "For even your kinsfolk and your own family,
>> even they have dealt treacherously with you;
>> they are in full cry after you;
> do not believe them,
>> though they speak friendly words to you. (Jer. 12:6, NRSV)

> Therefore thus says YHWH concerning the people of Anathoth, who seek your life, and say, 'You shall not prophesy in the name of YHWH, or you will die by our hand'— therefore thus says YHWH of hosts: I am going to punish them; the young men shall die by the sword; their sons and their daughters shall die by famine; and not even a remnant shall be left of them. For I will bring disaster upon the people of Anathoth, the year of their punishment." (Jer. 11:21-23, NRSV)

For readers of the New Testament, it was the audience's familiarity with this account in Jeremiah that provided the background for Jesus' allusion to Jeremiah when Jesus said, "Truly I tell you, no prophet is accepted in the prophet's hometown." (Luke 4:24, NRSV)

Jeremiah had a definite sense of being called by YHWH. His prophetic office was not something that he chose of his own volition but a vocation that was chosen for him. The objection that Jeremiah makes to YHWH during his call is a typical element in the standard "call narrative" for prophets:

> "Now the word of YHWH came to me saying,
>
>> 'Before I formed you in the womb I knew you,
>>
>> and before you were born I consecrated you;
>>
>> I appointed you a prophet to the nations.'

Then I said, 'Ah, Lord YHWH! Truly I do not know how to speak, for I am only a boy.' But YHWH said to me,

> 'Do not say, 'I am only a boy';
>
> for you shall go to all to whom I send you,
>
> and you shall speak whatever I command you,
>
> Do not be afraid of them,
>
> for I am with you to deliver you,
>
> says YHWH.'" (Jer. 1:4-8, NRSV)

What is unique with Jeremiah is the continual struggle that he expresses with his call and his mission. He asserts, "But I have not run away from being a shepherd in your service" (Jer. 17:16, NRSV), presumably because there were many occasions where such a reaction was either warranted or contemplated. YHWH has to repeat his charge to Jeremiah on multiple occasions in varied ways, such as, "But you, gird up your loins; stand up and tell them everything that I command you. Do not break down before them, or I will break you before them." (Jer. 1:17, NRSV)

Most scholars date Jeremiah's call to 627 B.C., which is often given as the date for Jeremiah's birth. The question relates to how one interprets the superscription at the beginning of the book. The verses under consideration read as follows:

> "The words of Jeremiah son of Hilkiah, of the priests who were in Anathoth in the land of Benjamin, to whom the word of YHWH came in the days of King Josiah son of Amon of Judah, in the thirteenth year of his reign. It came also in the days of King Jehoiakim son of Josiah of Judah, and until the end of the eleventh year of King Zedekiah son of Josiah of Judah, until the captivity of Jerusalem in the fifth month." (Jer. 1:1-3, NRSV)

This superscription clearly designates a period of time, beginning in one specific year and ending in another. Because of the reference to "the word of YHWH," most scholars interpret this superscription to refer to the length of Jeremiah's prophetic ministry. William Holladay, however, notes that there are absolutely no oracles or narrative accounts dated to Josiah's reign. The information for the superscription most likely comes from the oracle contained in Jer. 25:3: "For twenty-three years, from the thirteenth year of King Josiah son of Amon of Judah, to this day, {the word of the LORD has come to me,} and I have spoken persistently to you, {but you have not listened.}" The words marked in brackets do not appear in Baruch's shorter (Septuagint) version. If Holladay is right, this means Jeremiah is referencing not the date of his prophetic calling but rather the date of his birth.

The idea that Jeremiah believed he was called as a prophet since birth is certainly in line with the prophet's own words. He says, Now the word of the LORD came to me saying, 'Before I formed you in the womb I knew you, and before you were born I consecrated you; I appointed you a prophet to the nations.'" (Jer. 1:4-5, NRSV). This interpretation helps to explain not only the lack of any oracles or narratives dating to Josiah's reign but also the relationship of Jeremiah to Deuteronomy. Deuteronomy was not newly discovered six years into Jeremiah's ministry but while Jeremiah was still a child.

Chapter 4: Jeremiah's Bible

The intimate connection between the prophet Jeremiah and the book of Deuteronomy can hardly be overstated. The connection is so strong, in fact, that in the 19th century some critical scholars believed that Jeremiah was one of the authors of Deuteronomy itself. The importance of Deuteronomy (4-28) for Judeans in the last quarter of the 7th century B.C. has already been explained.

The Song of Moses (Ex. 32) was clearly another heavy influence on Jeremiah. Most scholars consider this text to be quite early and to antedate even the core material in Deuteronomy that traces back to the reforms of Hezekiah. From the Song of Moses, Jeremiah developed the view of the wilderness period as a type of honeymoon period between the nation and YHWH. He says:

"Thus says the LORD:

I remember the devotion of your youth,

your love as a bride,

how you followed me in the wilderness,

in a land not sown.

Israel was holy to the LORD,

the first fruits of his harvest." (Jer. 2:2-3, NRSV)

This view of the wilderness period is clearly different from later perspectives when the wilderness period was viewed as a time of apostasy.

In addition to Deuteronomy, Jeremiah is clearly dependent on the Psalms for much of his material. The implication is that Jeremiah read the Psalms and knew them well so that he could incorporate them into his preaching. The question then becomes how many of the psalms

Jeremiah had at his disposal, and what the form was in which these psalms appeared. Holladay has studied this question thoroughly and arrived at the conclusion that Jeremiah used Books I-III of the current Psalms collection. The book of Psalms is divided into five parts, each of which closes with a concluding doxology: Book I (1-41); Book II (42-72); Book III (73-89); Book IV (90-106); and Book V (107-150) (Anderson, 1983, 22). Holladay's conclusion, based on Jeremiah's internal references to the various psalms, is corroborated further by the material evidence provided by the Dead Sea Scrolls, which indicates that an early collection of psalms ending at Psalm 89 was stabilized earlier than the more fluid elements of Books IV and V.

Chapter 5: Jeremiah and His Personal Laments

As a priest not associated with the temple, much of the cultic ritual that Jeremiah would have been exposed to growing up in his priestly family was the performance and recitation of psalms. The book of Psalms contains two general types of laments. There are the communal or corporate laments, where the perspective is the first person plural and the lament decries corporate sin and wrongdoing and corporate punishment. The laments then ask for national or corporate salvation as a result of the repentance of the population reflected in the lament. Jeremiah invokes this form for: his drought liturgy (14:1-9); his laments on behalf of exiled kings (22:10, 28-30); his lament for the slain of Judah (8:22-9:2); and his lament for all of creation (9:10-11).

The second category consists of the individual or personal laments, which provide a first person singular perspective. These laments mourn personal sin and suffering and ask for personal salvation from the deity. Jeremiah is unique among the Hebrew prophets in making extensive use of this poetic form. Scholars have lumped these individual laments together into a collective group that they call "the Confessions of Jeremiah" (10:23-24; 11:18-12:6; 15:10-21; 17:9-10, 14-18; 18:19-23; and 20:7-12). These "Confessions" generated a large number of studies in the early 20th century that centered on the psychology of Jeremiah.

These are the some of the texts that led to Jeremiah's epithet of the "weeping prophet." The number of passages in these "Confessions", and even throughout the rest of the book of Jeremiah that concern weeping or crying, is quite high (Jer. 8:21; 9:1, 18; 13:17; 14:17; 22:10; 48:31). Using this medium, the prophet expresses a wide variety of complaints. One of the commands that YHWH issued to Jeremiah was that he was not allowed the comfort provided by a wife and children: "The word of YHWH came to me: You shall not take a wife, nor shall you have sons or daughters in this place" (Jer. 16:1-2, NRSV). As a result, the prophet cries out that he is lonely:

> "I did not sit in the company of merrymakers,
>
>> nor did I rejoice;
>
> under the weight of your hand I sat alone,
>
>> for you had filled me with indignation." (Jer. 15:17, NRSV)

Another theme that Jeremiah complains incessantly about is the enemies who surround him and plot against him. He says:

> "Then they said, 'Come, let us make plots against Jeremiah—for instruction shall not perish from the priest, nor counsel from the wise, nor the word from the prophet. Come, let us bring charges against him, and let us not heed any of his words.'" (Jer. 18:18, NRSV)

Depiction of Jeremiah weeping

Chapter 6: Jeremiah and False Prophecy

One of the earliest extant dated oracles from Jeremiah's career is the Temple Sermon (Jer. 7:2-15). Although this text itself does not provide a date for the speech, the related prose description in chapter 26 that summarizes this speech in a much more abbreviated form dates the event to the accession year of King Jehoiakim, 609 B.C. Jeremiah went to the entrance to the temple and proclaimed that its fate would be akin to that of the ancient sanctuary Shiloh. Although the Hebrew Bible nowhere describes the destruction of Shiloh directly, it is clear that with the destruction and subsequent deportation of the population of Israel by Sargon II, the Assyrians destroyed the ancient shrine at Shiloh. But Jeremiah was not unique in emphasizing the significance of the destruction of this ancient shrine. One of the psalms of Asaph, identified above as part of Jeremiah's Bible, makes a similar allusion to the destruction of this ancient cultic sanctuary: "He abandoned his dwelling at Shiloh, / the tent where he dwelt among mortals" (Ps. 78:60, NRSV).

The temple-going audience wanted no part of the dark picture that Jeremiah was painting for them and their temple. They seized him, accused him of false prophecy, and brought him before the princes (officials) who would judge the case (Jer. 26:8-9). This question of prophetic authenticity was a big one for Jeremiah and the other Hebrew prophets who engaged in this type of intuitive prophecy. Jeremiah himself at several points highlights the problem of false prophecy, at one point saying, "An appalling and horrible thing / has happened in the land: / the prophets prophesy falsely, / and the priests rule as the prophets direct" (Jer. 5:30-31, NRSV).

This problem of false prophecy had dire consequences, as Jeremiah indicated by the sentence he passed on such false prophets later in his career:

> "Then I said: 'Ah, Lord YHWH! Here are the prophets saying to them, 'You shall not see the sword, nor shall you have famine, but I will give you true peace in this place.' And YHWH said to me: The prophets are prophesying lies in my name; I did not send them, nor did I command them or speak to them. They are prophesying to you a lying vision, worthless divination, and the deceit of their own minds. Therefore thus says YHWH concerning the prophets who prophesy in my name though I did not send them, and who say, 'Sword and famine shall not come on this land': By sword and famine those prophets shall be consumed. And the people to whom they prophesy shall be thrown out into the streets of Jerusalem, victims of famine and sword. There shall be no one to bury them— themselves, their wives, their sons, and their daughters. For I will pour out their wickedness upon them." (Jer. 14:13-16, NRSV)

There was apparently a clear legal procedure for adjudicating such allegations. The plaintiffs, made up of priests and other prophets, formally recited the charges against Jeremiah (26:11). As the defendant, Jeremiah appealed to the third of the Deuteronomic criteria for discerning a true prophet (Deut. 18:22), that the prophet was sent by YHWH and not acting on his own volition (Jer. 26:12-15). Sitting in judgment, the princes cite a precedent where a former prophet (Micah of Moresheth) gave a prophecy of judgment against the temple but was not condemned because the courts judged his message to have been divinely inspired (Jer. 26:16-19). The plaintiffs (presumably) also respond with the counter precedent of Uriah of Kiriath-jearim, who was killed for his prophecy of judgment (Jer. 26:20-23). The fact that a friend of Jeremiah had to intervene and prevent him from receiving the death penalty suggests that this counter precedent was given the greatest weight in the case.

Later in his career, Jeremiah himself would pass judgment on another false prophet. A prophet named Shemaiah of Nehelam contradicted Jeremiah's words to the Babylonian exiles. He and all his children would die prematurely.

> "Then the word of YHWH came to Jeremiah: 'Send to all the exiles, saying, Thus says YHWH concerning Shemaiah of Nehelam: Because Shemaiah has prophesied to you, though I did not send him, and has led you to trust in a lie,' therefore thus says YHWH: 'I am going to punish Shemaiah of Nehelam and his descendants; he shall not have anyone living among this people to see the good that I am going to do to my people, says YHWH, for he has spoken rebellion against YHWH.'" (Jer. 29:30-32, NRSV)

One striking feature about the book of Jeremiah is that although it went through an extensive editing process, it retains both contradictory prophecies as well as unfulfilled prophecies. An example of the former are the numerous prophecies Jeremiah made concerning Zedekiah's fate, none of which match the fate described in gory detail in the book of Kings (2 Kgs. 25). At various points, Jeremiah prophesies that Zedekiah will: 1) die by the sword (20:1-7); 2) not die by the sword, but in peace (34:4-5); 3) inevitably be captured (34:21-22; 37:17); 4) inevitably be exiled (24:1-10; 32:3-5); 5) determine whether he will be captured and exiled by his actions (38:14-23). An example of the latter occurs with Jeremiah's prediction that there would be mass desecration of graves and exhumation of bodies in Jerusalem (Jer. 8:1-3). Such an event never came to pass.

Chapter 7: Jeremiah's Politics

At the core of Jeremiah's politics was a pro-Babylonian stance coupled with an anti-Egyptian framework. Jeremiah apparently got along with Josiah fairly well and even composed a lament for the occasion of his death (2 Chr. 35:25). Because of the political turmoil that the usual major political players were facing during his reign, Josiah was given a level of political freedom and independence that neither his predecessors nor those who followed him on the throne would enjoy. Between this and the common training the two had received in the Deuteronomic tradition, they were bound to be close allies. It was then heartbreaking for Jeremiah when Pharaoh Necho II took Shallum, Josiah's son, captive to Egypt of all places (Jer. 22:10-12). Pharaoh Necho II appointed Shallum's brother, Jehoiakim, to the throne instead of Shallum, and Jeremiah and King Jehoiakim rarely saw eye-to-eye on anything.

An Ancient Egyptian statue believed to be Necho II kneeling.

Jeremiah had many powerful political allies. Baruch ben Neriah, the scribe who worked closely with Jeremiah throughout his career, was an official scribe of the royal administration. Jeremiah was also closely associated with the children of two officials who had figured prominently in the Josianic reform: Shaphan, the royal secretary who had brought the book of the law to Josiah's attention, and Achbor, who had accompanied Shaphan when he visited the prophetess Huldah to help authenticate the book of the law. One of Shaphan's sons, Ahikam, helped Jeremiah escape what would surely have been a death sentence after his Temple Sermon (Jer. 26:24). Another of Shapan's sons, Elasah, carried Jeremiah's letters to the Babylonian exiles (Jer. 29:3). A third son of Shaphan, Gemariah, opened up his home for the reading of

Jeremiah's scroll, where Elnathan, the son of Achbor, sat as a sympathetic listener (Jer. 36:10-12).

In Jeremiah's eyes, the Babylonian King Nebuchadnezzar II was the instrument through which YHWH would act to deliver his judgment (Jer. 25:9). Jehoiakim, on the other hand, was pro-Egyptian. Although he paid his requisite tribute to Nebuchadnezzar, he was just waiting for the right opportunity to overthrow the Babylonian oppressors, who were in his eyes no better than the Assyrians to whom Manasseh had paid tribute.

An engraving on an eye stone of onyx with an inscription of Nebuchadnezzar II.

In 605 B.C., the momentous Battle of Carchemish took place between the Egyptian and Babylonian armies. Jeremiah prophesied that the Babylonians, along with the tribes of the north, would come against Judah and utterly destroy it (Jer. 25). He also delivered an oracle against Egypt on the occasion of the Battle of Carchemish (Jer. 46:1-12). Neither of these prophecies could have pleased Jehoiakim very much.

It was not only matters of foreign policy upon which Jehoiakim and Jeremiah disagreed. They also differed in their convictions regarding domestic policy as well. Jehoiakim conscripted a labor force to build a new royal palace for himself. One Hebrew seal from this period boasts the following inscription: "Belonging to Palayahu, who is over the compulsory labor". Jeremiah first lambasts Jehoiakim for his use of this conscripted labor force.

> "Woe to him who builds his house by unrighteousness,
>
> > and his upper rooms by injustice;
>
> who makes his neighbors work for nothing,
>
> > and does not give them their wages;

who says, 'I will build myself a spacious house

with large upper rooms,'" (Jer. 22:13-14, NRSV)

But Jeremiah did not stop there. It is not merely the means that Jehoiakim was using to build his new palace that bothered him but the materials with which he chose to furnish it. Cedar was the building material of choice for royal palaces, but it came out of Lebanon. Nebuchadnezzar had just subdued this area of Syria/Lebanon and was marching about victoriously in it. He was then importing the cedar from Lebanon into Babylon for his many royal building projects. Jeremiah, therefore, accuses Jehoiakim of trying to be like Nebuchadnezzar.

"and who cuts out windows for it,

paneling it with cedar,

and painting it with vermilion.

Are you a king

because you compete in cedar?" (Jer. 22:14-15, NRSV)

Jeremiah's next move is to compare Jehoiakim to his father, knowing full well that the son would not want to be judged as inferior to his father:

"Did not your father eat and drink

and do justice and righteousness?

Then it was well with him.

He judged the cause of the poor and needy;

then it was well.

Is not this to know me?

says YHWH." (Jer. 22:15-16, NRSV)

His final rhetorical flourish is to pronounce a curse upon Jehoiakim for his actions of greed and oppression.

"But your eyes and heart

are only on your dishonest gain,

for shedding innocent blood,

and for practicing oppression and violence.

Therefore thus says YHWH concerning King Jehoiakim son of Josiah of Judah:

They shall not lament for him, saying,

'Alas, my brother!" or "Alas, sister!'

They shall not lament for him, saying,

'Alas, lord!" or "Alas, his majesty!'

With the burial of a donkey he shall be buried—

dragged off and thrown out beyond the gates of Jerusalem."

(Jer. 22:17-19, NRSV)

Despite what would appear to be repeated calls for the assassination of Jehoiakim, no one was willing to take it that far. When Jehoiakim took note of the internal turmoil that was taking place in Babylon itself, combined with the external threat of Egypt that had inflicted major losses on the Babylonian army, he decided it was time to act. In the year 600 B.C., he defied Nebuchadnezzar and refused to make his annual tribute payment. Jehoiakim had timed his act of rebellion well, and Nebuchadnezzar was in no shape to take immediate and swift action against Judah for their defiance. Faced with Jehoiakim's act of defiance, Nebuchadnezzar wanted to act swiftly, but he knew he had his hands full with other pressing matters. As a stopgap measure, he encouraged the small city-states surrounding Judah, including the Aramaeans, the Ammonites and the Moabites, to attack Judah with his blessing (2 Kgs. 24:2).

A Renaissance depiction of Jehoiakim

It wasn't until the following year, his seventh year on the throne (597 BC), that Nebuchadnezzar decided to deal with Judah and the city of Jerusalem directly. He marched his army to Ḥatti late in the year, as was his new custom, and besieged Jerusalem. For those in Jerusalem, as had been the case with Ekron a few years earlier, the expected aid from Egypt never came.

By the time Nebuchadnezzar captured the city, Jehoiakim was dead, and Jehoiachin, his 18-year old son and heir, was on the throne. Jehoiachin, who had only reigned in Jerusalem for three months before it was overrun by the Babylonian army, would pay for his father's actions. Jehoiachin was carried off captive to Babylon along with his family and 10,000 soldiers, mechanics and ruling elites in the city, including the Judean prophet Ezekiel. This was the second of three deportations the Judeans would face at the hands of Nebuchadnezzar.

In addition to carrying off people, Nebuchadnezzar helped himself to some of the vessels in the Jewish temple, bringing them to Babylon and dedicating them to Marduk. As part of his efforts to keep the region under his control, Nebuchadnezzar then installed a king of his own. The Babylonian king appointed Mattaniah, Jehoiakim's brother, as a puppet, and Mattaniah took the throne name Zedekiah.

Jeremiah's relationship with Zedekiah was slightly less strained than his relationship had been with Jehoiakim. This should not come as a complete surprise, in light of Jeremiah's pro-

Babylonian stance and the fact that Nebuchadnezzar had handpicked Zedekiah to sit on the Judean throne. At the same time, this more amicable relationship did not stop Jeremiah from prophesying about Zedekiah's death and destruction on numerous occasions. Shortly after he secured the throne, Zedekiah assembled an anti-Babylonian summit in Jerusalem. In response to this, Jeremiah made a yoke that he would put on himself every time he ventured out into public over the next four years. His message to Zedekiah from YHWH was that if the king submitted to the yoke of the Babylonians, he would continue to live on his land.

In 594 B.C., Zedekiah made a conciliatory trip to Babylon to assure Nebuchadnezzar of his loyalty after having organized an anti-Babylonian summit in Jerusalem just a few years earlier in 597. Jeremiah offered to help Zedekiah with this foreign relations trip based on his pro-Babylonian politics. He wrote two letters for this trip. One public letter appears in chapter 29 and was intended for the Judean exiles in Babylon. The other was a private letter with an oracle asserting that Babylon would fall completely, which he entrusted to Seraiah, Baruch's brother, who would accompany Zedekiah on the journey. Seraiah was to read it aloud and toss it into the Euphrates River, thus beginning the countdown to Babylon's destruction.

When Nebuchadnezzar finally besieged the city a few years later in 586 B.C., Jeremiah attempted to leave the city through a breach in the wall. According to Jeremiah, he just had to leave while the city was under siege to buy a field in his hometown, Anathoth. This was an action that may have well been rendered entirely ineffectual given the current military situation in the city. The royal guards who caught him had a different interpretation of his actions. They accused him of deserting to the Babylonians (Jer. 37). Jeremiah denied it, but it is not very hard to see why his story would seem quite fishy. He was then beaten and put in prison. Zedekiah felt pity on him and also wanted to procure his prophetic services, so he allowed Jeremiah to move from prison to house arrest. He then began preaching surrender, which got him thrown into a cistern. There he would have died had it not been for the kindness of an Ethiopian named Ebed-melech. When Nebuchadnezzar seized the upper classes and deported them to Babylon, Jeremiah was spared this fate because of his political views and allowed to remain in the land. As much as he favored the Babylonians, there was no place like home.

In the aftermath of the destruction of Jerusalem, a new government was formed in Mizpah under the leadership of Gedaliah, now called "governor" instead of "king." Jeremiah joined them in Mizpah, but shortly thereafter, Gedaliah was assassinated (Jer. 40-41). When the people with him turned to Jeremiah for a word from YHWH, he remained silent for 10 days. After that, he prophesied that they should remain in the land. However, they dismissed his message and a group traveled to Egypt for safety, bringing Baruch and Jeremiah with them (Jer. 43:7).

Chapter 8: Jeremiah's Theology

Jeremiah conveys a uniquely intimate relationship with YHWH in his oracles and confessions. He experiences the full range of emotions directed toward the deity that one would express to a very close friend or to a spouse. He expresses anger, longing, and frustration toward YHWH. He declares his great love for YHWH in one breath and then accuses YHWH in another. On the one hand, YHWH is "the fountain of living water" (Jer. 2:13). On the other hand, he is "like a deceitful brook, like waters that fail" (Jer. 15:18). At other times, his accusations of deceit do not rely on the more gentle language of the simile: "Then I said, 'Ah, Lord YHWH, how utterly you have deceived this people and Jerusalem, saying, 'It shall be well with you,' even while the sword is at the throat!'" (Jer. 4:10, NRSV). In one instance he warns YHWH, "Do not become a terror to me" (Jer. 17:17, NRSV).

Naturally, Jeremiah gives praise to YHWH and looks to him for healing: "Heal me, O YHWH, and I shall be healed; / save me, and I shall be saved; / for you are my praise" (Jer. 17:14, NRSV). But then he turns around and accuses YHWH of poisoning his own people, "for YHWH our God has doomed us to perish, / and has given us poisoned water to drink" (Jer. 8:14, NRSV; see also Jer. 9:15).

Although he was trained in the Deuteronomic school of thought, his theology is much more developed than that apparent in Deuteronomy. For the Deuteronomists, everything was black and white. Part of the impetus behind the composition of the book of Job, written several centuries later, was to question the black-and-white view espoused by the Deuteronomists. It is common in modern contemporary speech to differentiate between "spirituality" and "religion," with the former being more experiential and the latter more rule-based. Jeremiah's theology was clearly more "spiritual" and relational in nature, as opposed to the more rule-based Deuteronomic theology.

Chapter 9: Jeremiah and Sex

The book of Jeremiah is filled with sexual imagery, and in order to fully understand the prophet, it is necessary to examine some of what he has to say about sex. Jeremiah frequently accuses Israel and Judah of acting as a prostitute. In one instance, he describes in detail the clothing and accoutrements that a prostitute would wear to seduce a lover, but then chastens Judah that such preparations would be in vain anyway because her Johns hate her.

> "And you, O desolate one,
>
> what do you mean that you dress in crimson,
>
> > that you deck yourself with ornaments of gold,
> >
> > that you enlarge your eyes with paint?
>
> In vain you beautify yourself.
>
> > Your lovers despise you;

they seek your life." (Jer. 4:30)

Jeremiah's language was provocative, and rhetorical flourishes for effect were part of his stock-in-trade. In his references to sexual imagery, Jeremiah even uses profanity to underscore the emotional nature of his divine message to the people of Judah. In chapter 3, Jeremiah personifies the Northern Kingdom of Israel as a whore:

> What does it say,[i] "If a man divorces his wife,
>
> > and she goes from him
>
> and marries another man,
>
> > will he return to her again?
>
> Will not that land surely be polluted?
>
> Although, you have screwed many lovers;
>
> > nevertheless, you (expect to) return to me?" oracle of YHWH.
>
> Lift up your eyes to the barren roads and look!
>
> > Where have you not been f***ed?[ii]
>
> Upon the waysides you have sat waiting for them,
>
> > like an Arab in the wilderness.
>
> You have defiled the land
>
> > with your promiscuity and wickedness."
>
> (Jer. 3:1-2)

Jeremiah begins by citing Israel's legal tradition contained in Deuteronomy 24:1-4, which talks about the case of a divorce where a woman remarries but then divorces her second husband as well. But Jeremiah merely uses this as a starting point. The picture he wants to convey to his audience is far more graphic. Whereas the woman in the legal case has only had sexual relations (presumably) with two ex-husbands, Jeremiah accuses the land of Israel of having many lovers. He then extends the rhetorical point further by asking Israel to look around at the "barren roads." The Hebrew term is intentionally ambiguous, meaning both "mountain tracks" where travelers frequent and prostitutes often plied their trade, as well as "high places" where Israel would frequently erect altars for worshipping other gods according to the Deuteronomistic historian.

This concept is paralleled in another of Jeremiah's oracles, where he says, "On every *high hill* and under every green tree you sprawled and played the whore." (Jer. 2:20, NRSV).

For pious believers, both Christians and Jews, such a suggestion that the prophet was using profanity seems quite scandalous. But a quick check of even the most conservative commentaries on the book of Jeremiah will note that this word is profane. It was even considered profane by the medieval Jews who copied the Hebrew text. In fact, it was so profane that the scribes added a note to the text whenever this passage was read in the synagogue to ensure a more tame euphemism added to the margin would be read rather than this profane word. Using the same conventions already established for reading the divine name, the scribes distinguished between what was actually written in the text and what was to be read aloud. Modern English translations of the Bible retain this Jewish tradition and translate the marginal reading, like the NRSV "Where have you not been lain with?" to avoid offending pious readers of the sacred text. This profane word appears on three other occasions in the Hebrew Bible, each of which is an unsavory sexual context (Deut. 28:30; Is. 13:16; Zech. 14:2).

In another context, Jeremiah is issuing an oracle of judgment against the city Jerusalem. At one point in the oracle, Jeremiah anticipates that the inhabitants of the city may be asking themselves why this particular judgment is falling upon them. Jeremiah's response is that their fate is a result of their unacceptable behavior.

> "And if you say in your heart,
>
>> 'Why have these things come upon me?'
>
> it is for the greatness of your iniquity
>
>> that your skirts are lifted up,
>
>> and you are violated." (Jer. 13:22, NRSV)

Here Jeremiah uses language that compares Jerusalem's fate to that of a rape victim. These same words are echoed by Jeremiah just a few lines later in this same judgment oracle, but within an entirely different context.

> "This is your lot,
>
>> the portion I have measured out to you, says YHWH,
>
> because you have forgotten me
>
>> and trusted in lies.
>
> I myself will lift up your skirts over your face,

and your shame will be seen." (Jer. 13:25-26, NRSV)

Although Jeremiah uses the same image of a woman's skirt being lifted up in both couplets, the first evokes the image of a woman being raped, whereas the second evokes the image of a woman being divorced. This type of sexual shaming was a typical element of divorce proceedings in the ancient Near East. One Old Assyrian law explains that a man may strip his unfaithful wife and chase her out of the house naked.

In another of his laments, Jeremiah has no qualms about casting YHWH as a sexual assailant (and some would even say rapist). In one lamentation he cries out:

> "O YHWH, you seduced me,
>
> and I was seduced;
>
> you overpowered me,
>
> and you prevailed.
>
> I have become a laughingstock all day long;
>
> everyone mocks me.
>
> For whenever I speak, I cry out,
>
> I shout, 'Violence and destruction!'
>
> For the word of YHWH has become for me
>
> a reproach and derision all day long.
>
> If I say, 'I will not mention him,
>
> or speak any more in his name,'
>
> then within me there is something like a burning fire
>
> shut up in my bones;
>
> I am weary with holding it in,
>
> and I cannot." (Jer. 20:7-9)

Jeremiah is describing his calling by YHWH as an event that he could not say "no" to any more than a woman being raped could say "no" to her assailant. This lament evokes the legal material contained in Deut. 22:22-29, which articulates the legal precedent for a woman who is raped. The legal material in Deuteronomy makes much of whether the woman cried out or not. In Jeremiah's lament, he emphasizes that he cried out, but that rather than obtaining justice with his cries, he received only ridicule and derision, probably a common fate of rape victims in his day as well.

Chapter 9: Jeremiah and His Enemies

In the "Confessions" of Jeremiah, he frequently cries out to YHWH about his enemies, but it is clear that he is not content to simply let YHWH decide what their fate should be. He has no qualms about uttering prophetic curses against his enemies that he believed YHWH would enact upon them on his behalf. Some of these are very general in their tone and in the punishment that will befall his enemies. These are the types of curses that one might expect to come from a messenger of God.

> "But YHWH is with me like a dread warrior;
>
>> therefore my persecutors will stumble,
>
>> and they will not prevail.
>
> They will be greatly shamed,
>
>> for they will not succeed.
>
> Their eternal dishonor
>
>> will never be forgotten." (Jer. 20:11, NRSV)

At some points he clarifies that he does not want the curses he pronounces upon his enemies to fall on him.

> "Let my persecutors be shamed,
>
>> but do not let me be shamed;
>
> let them be dismayed,
>
>> but do not let me be dismayed;
>
> bring on them the day of disaster;
>
>> destroy them with double destruction!" (Jer. 17:18)

In one instance, Jeremiah goes head-to-head with the chief priest and fellow prophet,

Hananiah. One of his prophetic devices that he had been using was to bind a yoke on himself whenever he went into public as a picture of the yoke of the Babylonians to which the Judeans needed to submit. One day, Hananiah received a word from YHWH, and in a prophetic act of his own he broke the yoke off of Jeremiah's neck and declared:

> "Thus says YHWH of hosts, the God of Israel: I have broken the yoke of the king of Babylon. Within two years I will bring back to this place all the vessels of YHWH'S house, which King Nebuchadnezzar of Babylon took away from this place and carried to Babylon. I will also bring back to this place King Jeconiah son of Jehoiakim of Judah, and all the exiles from Judah who went to Babylon, says YHWH, for I will break the yoke of the king of Babylon." (Jer. 28:2-4, NRSV)

In the heat of the moment, Jeremiah affirmed Hananiah's contradictory message. But just a little while later, YHWH confirmed to Jeremiah his original message. This put Jeremiah in the awkward position of cursing his colleague and friend in the same way that he would curse his enemies.

> "Listen, Hananiah, YHWH has not sent you, and you made this people trust in a lie. Therefore, thus says YHWH: I am going to send you off the face of the earth. Within this year you will be dead, because you have spoken rebellion against YHWH." (Jer. 28:15-16)

The narrator notes that Hananiah died in the seventh month of that year.

On the other hand, there are some cases where Jeremiah's language is quite disturbing in its graphic detail.

> "Give heed to me, O YHWH,
>
>> and listen to what my adversaries say!
>
> Is evil a recompense for good?
>
>> Yet they have dug a pit for my life.
>
> Remember how I stood before you
>
>> to speak good for them,
>
>> to turn away your wrath from them.
>
> Therefore give their children over to famine;

> hurl them out to the power of the sword,
>
> let their wives become childless and widowed.
>
> May their men meet death by pestilence,
>
> their youths be slain by the sword in battle.
>
> May a cry be heard from their houses,
>
> when you bring the marauder suddenly upon them!"
>
> (Jer. 18:19-22, NRSV)

The imagery is descriptive, but it shows a very human side of the prophet. It is notable that this curse is not attributed to an "oracle of YHWH" or introduced with "thus says YHWH," but is written in the style of Jeremiah's Confessions that express the prophet's own views and emotions as they are directed toward YHWH.

Chapter 10: Jeremiah and His Apprentice

By all accounts, Baruch the scribe worked very closely with Jeremiah. When Jeremiah was unable to enter the temple himself, he sent Baruch to read his message for him. In fact, the relationship between Jeremiah and the scribe Baruch was so close that some of the Judeans accused Jeremiah of being the messenger not of YHWH but of Baruch.

> "Azariah son of Hoshaiah and Johanan son of Kareah and all the other insolent men said to Jeremiah, 'You are telling a lie. YHWH our God did not send you to say, 'Do not go to Egypt to settle there'; but Baruch son of Neriah is inciting you against us, to hand us over to the Chaldeans, in order that they may kill us or take us into exile in Babylon.'" (Jer. 43:2-3, NRSV)

Later Jewish tradition makes Baruch out to be a prophet as well, most likely conceiving of him as possessing the same relationship to Jeremiah as Elisha had to Elijah in the 9th century B.C.

Chapter 11: Jeremiah's Fate

When Jeremiah was whisked away to Egypt, he continued his prophetic message there, and it is not surprising that he delivered an oracle against the nation of Egypt itself. He had delivered oracles against many other nations, so an oracle against his political nemesis would certainly be expected. Once that was out of the way, he turned his attention to the religious practices of the expatriate Jews living in Tahpanhes, where he had settled.

These Jews were worshipping a goddess that Jeremiah called the "Queen of Heaven." The most likely identification of this goddess is with Assyrian/Babylonian Ištar and West Semitic Astarte. This deity was called the "Queen of Heaven" in Akkadian and the "Lady of Heaven" in New Kingdom Egypt, a slight difference due to the fact the Egyptian language does not have close cognate terms in the way that Akkadian and Hebrew do. Even though Jeremiah is unique in his use of this term in the Hebrew Bible, there is one extant Hebrew letter written on papyrus found at ancient Hermopolis in 1945 that uses this same term. The letter dates from the late 6th century B.C., only shortly after Jeremiah's career. A portion of that letter read:

> "Greetings to the temple of Bethel and the temple of the Queen of Heaven.
>
> To my sister Nanaiham from your brother Nabusha.
>
> I bless you by Ptah—may he let me see you again in good health…
>
> The tunic you sent has arrived. I found it all streaked; I just don't like it at all! Do you have plenty of other kinds?…
>
> Don't worry about me…
>
> Greetings to my father…Greetings to my mother…"

Evidently, in going about their daily affairs, these Jews worshipped at the temple of the Queen of Heaven without even giving it a second thought. In their theological framework, the destruction of Jerusalem was a result of the cessation of the worship of the Queen of Heaven as a result of the Josianic/Deuteronomic reforms.

Jeremiah's words contained in chapter 44 are the last mention of him in the Hebrew Bible, but there is another tradition contained in the apocryphal/deuterocanonical book of Baruch (as well as several midrashic traditions) that Jeremiah was taken to Babylon. There is some scant evidence in the Babylonian records that Nebuchadnezzar attacked the Pharaoh Amasis in the 37th year of his reign. In the Jewish traditions, Nebuchadnezzar captured some of the Jews who had settled in the Nile Delta of Egypt for safety and deported them to Babylon as well. It is possible to connect the Babylonian records with the Jewish tradition, but there are no Egyptian records that would support this.

Jerome preserves two distinct oral traditions about Jeremiah's death that came down to him. According to one account, he was stoned (*Adversus Jovinianum*, 2:37), but according to a different tradition he died of natural causes (Lipiński, 2007, 129). It's likely that the death of Jeremiah by stoning was originally a Jewish tradition that passed down to the Christians as a form of martyrdom. Other traditions even go so far as to claim that Egypt celebrated Jeremiah for delivering them from a plague of mice, and that Jeremiah even met the famous Greek philosopher Plato.

Regardless of how he died, Jeremiah is still one of the most vivid figures in the Bible, and his book is still quotes frequently in a variety of contexts. The Deuteronomistic History (the scholarly name for the Former Prophets) was considered prophetic by Jews but not by Christians. This may reflect the fact that "history," an important concept in the Greek tradition, was not an important concept in Jewish/Hebrew thought. The history of Israel and Judah and the rise and fall of the monarchy was not interpreted by the Jewish people as a historical record of their past but rather as a prophetic message of salvation, divine punishment, and redemption.

Jeremiah, of course, came to embody all of that.

Bibliography

Anderson, Bernhard W. *Out of the Depths: The Psalms Speak for Us Today*. (Philadelphia, 1983).

Bright, John. *Jeremiah: A New Translation with Introduction and Commentary*. Garden City, NY, 1965).

Fishbane, Michael A. *Biblical Interpretation in Ancient Israel*. Oxford, 1985.

Flint, Peter W. "Psalms and Psalters in the Dead Sea Scrolls." Pp. 233-72 in James H. Charlesworth (ed.) *The Bible and the Dead Sea Scrolls. Vol. 1: Scripture and the Scrolls*. (Waco, TX, 2006).

Hillers, Delbert R. "Lamentations, The Book of." Vol. IV pp. 137-41 in David Noel Freedman (ed.) *The Anchor Bible Dictionary*. (New York, 1992).

Holladay, William L. *Jeremiah 1: A Commentary on the Book of the Prophet Jeremiah, Chapters 1-25* (Philadelphia, 1986).

Holladay, William L. "Indications of Jeremiah's Psalter." *Journal of Biblical Literature* 121 (2002) 245-61.

Houtman, C. "Queen of Heaven." Pp. 678-80 in Karel Van der Toorn, Bob Becking and Pieter van der Horst (eds.) *Dictionary of Deities and Demons in the Bible*. (Leiden, 1999).

Hyatt, J. Philip. "Jeremiah and Deuteronomy." *Journal of Near Eastern Studies* 1 (1942) 156-73.

Koch, Klaus. *The Prophets*. 2 Vols. (Philadelphia, 1982).

Leuchter, Mark. *Josiah's Reform and Jeremiah's Scroll: Historical Calamity and Prophetic Response*. (Sheffield, UK, 2006).

Lindenberger, James M. *Ancient Aramaic and Hebrew Letters*. 2nd Ed. (Atlanta, 2003).

Lipiński, Edward. "Jeremiah." Vol. 11 pp. 125-34 in Michael Berenbaum and Fred Skolnik (eds.) *Encyclopædia Judaica*. (Detroit, 2007).

Lundbom, Jack R. "Jeremiah (Prophet)." Vol. III pp. 684-98 in David Noel Freedman (ed.) *The Anchor Bible Dictionary*. (New York, 1992).

Lundbom, Jack R. "Jeremiah, Book of." Vol. III pp. 707-21 in David Noel Freedman (ed.) *The Anchor Bible Dictionary*. (New York, 1992).

Miller, J. Maxwell and John H. Hayes. *A History of Ancient Israel and Judah*. (Philadelphia, 1986)

Steiner, Richard C. "The Two Sons of Neraiah and the Two Editions of Jeremiah in the Light of Two Atbash Code-Words for Babylon." *Vetus Testamentum* 46 (1996) 74-84.

VanderKam, James and Peter Flint. *The Meaning of the Dead Sea Scrolls*. (San Francisco, 2004).

Van der Toorn, Karel. "From the Mouth of the Prophet: The Literary Fixation of Jeremiah's Prophecies in the Context of the Ancient Near East." Pp. 191-202 in John Kaltner and Louis Stulman (eds.) *Inspired Speech: Prophecy in the Ancient Near East: Essays in Honor of Herbert B. Huffmon*. (New York, 2004).

Veenhof, Klaas. "Old Assyrian Period." Pp. 431-84 in Raymond Westbrook (ed.) *A History of Ancient Near Eastern Law*. (Leiden, 2003)

Whitley, C. F. "The Date of Jeremiah's Call." *Vetus Testamentum* 14 (1964) 467-83.

---

[i] The translation of this phrase (one word in Hebrew) is based on Fishbane's (1985, 307) analysis of this passage,

where he notes that this word is used as a citation formula similar to the phrase "it is written" in New Testament Greek usage for citing scripture (the Old Testament).

[ii] Margaret Kohl proposed this translation of this line in her 1982 English translation of Klaus Koch's work *Die Propheten I: Assyrische Zeit.*

Made in the USA
Middletown, DE
10 December 2021

55102252R00022